THE MURDERS IN THE RUE MORGUE

EDGAR ALLAN POE

Retold by Gill Tavner

Illustrated by Felix Bennett

Ernst Klett Sprachen
Stuttgart

1. Auflage 1 [5 4 3 2 1] | 2017 16 15 14 13

This edition of The Murders in the Rue Morgue is published by arrangement with Real Reads Ltd.

First published in 2012

Internetadresse: www.klett.de / www.lektueren.com

Annotationen und Übungen: Joanne Popp

Redaktion: Don Haupt
Illustrationen: Felix Bennett
Gestaltung und Satz: Elmar Feuerbach
Umschlaggestaltung: Elmar Feuerbach
Titelgrafik: Felix Bennett
Druck und Bindung: Medienhaus Plump GmbH, Rolandsecker Weg 33, 53619 Rheinbreitbach
Printed in Germany

ISBN 978-3-12-542501-9

CONTENTS

THE CHARACTERS

Monsieur Auguste Dupin

Intrigued by two recent murders, this young man attempts to use his sharp analytical skills to discover what happened in the Rue Morgue.

The narrator

He is keen to set you a challenge, and invites you to pit *your* analytical skills against those of his friend, Dupin.

intrigued [ɪn'triːgd] interested – **to attempt sth** to try sth – **sharp** fast, clever, good – **narrator** sb who tells a story

You – the reader

How strong are your powers of analysis? Can you read minds? Can you beat Dupin to an explanation of the gruesome events in the Rue Morgue?

The murderer

Two brutal murders for which there is no apparent motive. Escape when there is no means of escape. The murderer has the police confounded.

A sailor

Why is he so anxious when he visits Dupin's apartment?

to beat sb to be faster than sb else, to defeat – **gruesome** ['gruːsəm] horrible, frightening – **apparent** sth that can be clearly seen – **means** way – **confounded** *here:* not knowing how to solve sth – **sailor** sb who works on boats – **anxious** ['æŋkʃəs] nervous and unsure of oneself

THE MURDERS IN THE RUE MORGUE

The world's most puzzling mysteries – what song the Syrens sang, for example, or what name Achilles assumed when he hid himself among women – can still be guessed at. They may even yet be solved.

Do you enjoy solving puzzles? Do you like crosswords, sudoku and logic puzzles? How about a game of chess or draughts? Maybe you enjoy working out 'whodunnit' in thrillers or detective stories before anyone else can.

If it's not something that you particularly enjoy, perhaps you know somebody who does. You may even know somebody who is extremely good at these sorts of things.

Quite often it seems to the rest of us that a person who is unusually good at puzzles, or is a good detective, is gifted with a sixth sense.

puzzling mystery problem that is hard to solve, but is interesting – **to assume** *here:* to use – **among** in the middle of – **draughts** [drɑːfts] *Dame (Spiel)* – **whodunnit** *(inf)* who has done it – **particularly** especially, very much

It seems as though they can just ‘feel’ the solution, as though they are ‘inspired’. We can imagine that their mind works a bit like this:

mysterious strange, unusual

However, recent experiences are leading me to believe that this is not the case. In fact, quite contradicting the theory of 'inspiration', I would now argue that the minds of such people depend more upon logic than upon inspiration, like this:

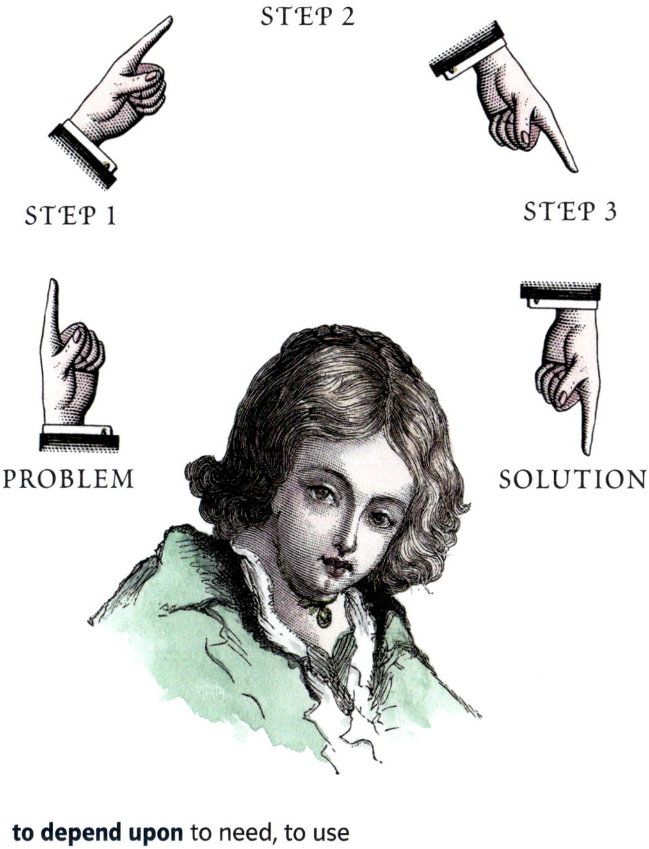

to depend upon to need, to use

Far from relying upon inspiration in working out puzzles, it seems that a skilful person works very methodically, progressing carefully, step by step, towards a conclusion. Do you agree with me? This method is called *analysis*. A person who excels in this is considered to have an *analytical mind*.

This process can be illustrated in the way many computer games work, where you have to gather equipment or information in order to work systematically towards a goal or destination. Consider the goal as the solution to the mystery, the equipment or information as the logical steps necessary to get there.

An analytical person enjoys the mental exercise of working things out as much as an athletic person enjoys the physical challenge of working out in a gym. Is this how you see things too? Do *you* enjoy working out difficult puzzles? Are *you* analytical?

Here is a test or, if you prefer, a puzzle for

to rely upon to make use of – **to progress** to move forward – **to excel** [ɪk'sel] to be very good at sth – **to gather** to collect, to look for – **in order to** to be able to – **destination** where you are going or wanting to go – **mental** using your head – **athletic person** sb who is sporty

you to work out, and I have to admit that it defeated me at the time. It is a faithful account of two most gruesome murders, in seemingly impossible circumstances. Can *you* work out what actually happened in the early hours of one fateful morning in the Rue Morgue?

faithful honest, true to the facts – **account** story – **circumstance** situation, time and place – **fateful** *schicksalhaft*

Before you start, here are a few tips. To be a good detective you need the same skills as a good card-player. You must consider and examine *every detail*, not just the obvious ones. You have to observe every change in a person's face, everything they say, everything they do. You must always expect the unexpected. And you must remember it all.

In this most strange tale, you'll see an analytical friend of mine at work as he progresses step by step towards a conclusion. Can you make faster progress than he was able to? Can you beat him to the solution of the mystery? I will present the evidence in the order in which we received it ourselves.

Some years ago I was living in Paris. At that time Paris was an ideal city in which to spend time observing the world and reading to one's heart's content, both of which I love to do.

tale story – **to one's heart's content** *nach Herzenslust*

I had the good fortune of meeting a gentleman called Monsieur Auguste Dupin. We met by chance in the library, where we were both searching for the same book. We started chatting, went for a coffee, and over time became great friends.

Poor Dupin seemed tired and sad. He told me that he came from a wealthy family, but a series of unfortunate events had led to the loss of most of his money. In spite of his sadness, he retained a lively mind and a fresh, vivid imagination. He was just the kind of friend I needed at that point in my life.

fortune ['fɔːtʃuːn] luck – **by chance** sth that wasn't planned – **wealthy** rich – **to retain** to keep – **lively** ['laɪvli] active, busy – **vivid imagination** *lebhafte Phantasie*

Renting an apartment together, we led a strange life. In the daytime, we shut the sunlight out and spent our time reading and talking by candlelight. When the real darkness of night-time fell we walked around Paris together, watching what people were doing and very often lost in our own thoughts.

You think this is odd? Is it so very different from sitting in the dark watching the television or going to the cinema? No, the way we chose to pass the time wasn't particularly odd, but this fact is – *Dupin could read my mind!*

As we walked through the quiet streets, he would from time to time break the silence with a low chuckle. When I looked to him for an explanation, he answered, 'I know what you're thinking about.' At such times he would have an expression of madness on his face, his body would become rigid, his eyes wild, and his voice tense and high-pitched.

to shut out to stop sth coming through – **to pass the time** to do sth so that time goes by – **to break the silence** to make a noise – **chuckle** ['tʃʌkl] laugh – **rigid** ['rɪdʒɪd] hard, stiff, not flexible – **tense and high-pitched** spoken nervously and in a voice higher than normal

The first few times he did this I was disbelieving and slightly uneasy. I would challenge him: 'So tell me then, what *am* I thinking?' Yet the more it happened, the more my disbelief was replaced by amazement, my unease by curiosity. He was always right. But how could he possibly read my mind?

Have you ever tried to follow your train of thoughts backwards to see what it was that made you think of something? For example, a person might accidentally bump into you in the street and you suddenly remember that you have a maths test on Monday. Where did that thought come from?

It might have followed a route like this:

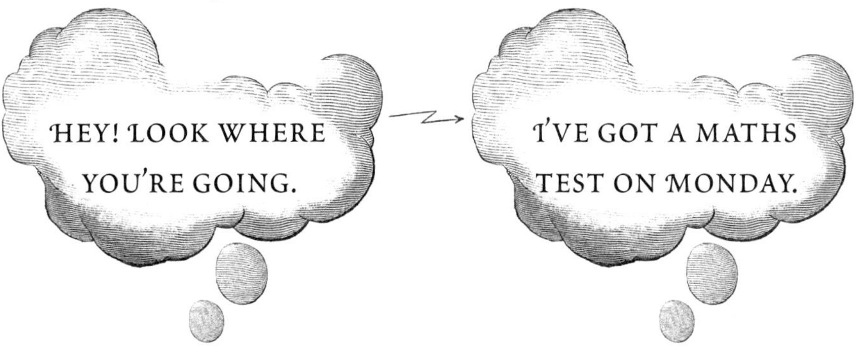

slightly uneasy not very comfortable or sure of sth – **amazement** surprise – **curiosity** [kjʊəriˈɒsəti] an eager wish to know about sth *(Neugier)* – **train of thought** the way sb is thinking, a series of connected thoughts – **accidentally** *versehentlich*

But that's not really very likely. It's more likely to have been like this:

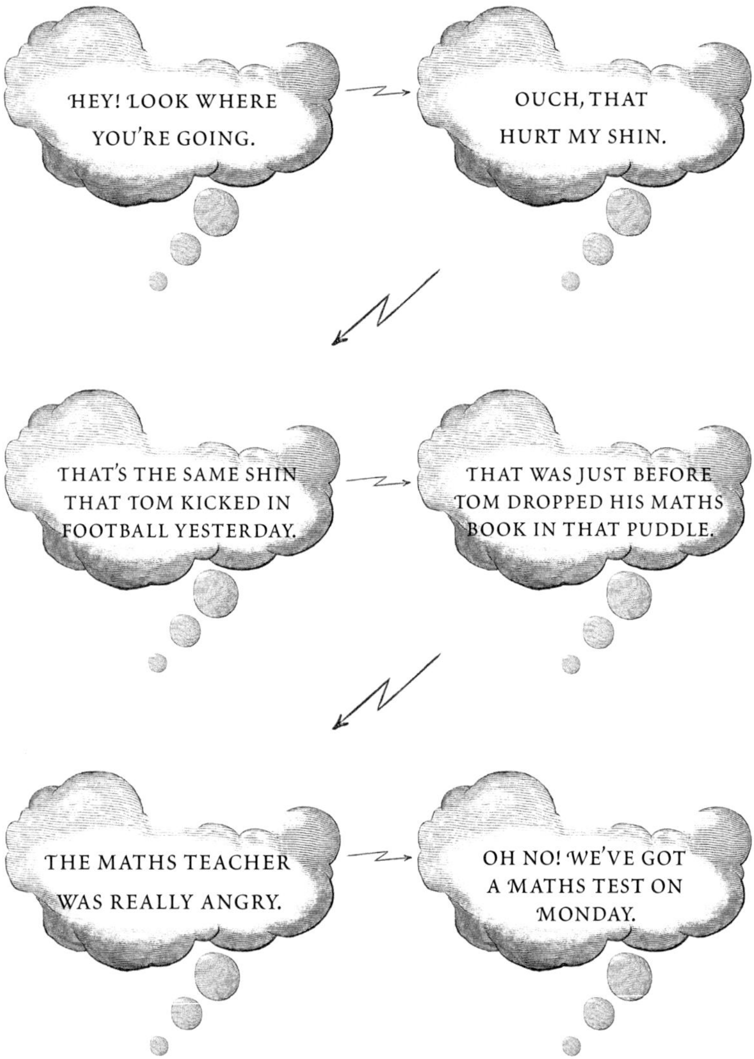

shin [ʃɪn] the front part of your leg below the knee – **puddle** ['pʌdl] a small pool of water, especially when it has rained

Thus, maybe in less than a second, your chain of thoughts has taken you from an unfortunate collision to Monday's maths test. Does that make sense to you?

This is how Dupin explained his ability to read my mind. He would notice an event and, watching me closely, use logic and his knowledge of my character to work out my train of thought. No sixth sense, no mystery, just very clever, methodical, *analytical* thinking.

Enough of maths tests. Here's *your* test, relating to a gruesome double murder which occurred during our time in Paris; two very strange murders with very few clues.

We first learned about the deaths of Madame and Mademoiselle L'Espanaye in our newspaper, the *Gazette des Tribunaux*. Remember that I have advised you to consider *every* detail.

collision [kəˈlɪʒn] crash, accident – **to make sense** to understand, to be logical – **ability** the skill to do sth – **to occur** [əˈkɜː] to happen, to take place – **clue** a tip or piece of information that helps you solve a problem

Murders in

The mutilated bodies of an elderly lady and her daughter have been discovered in their home in the Rue Morgue. Police are still interviewing witnesses, but at present have very few clues.

Horrific Shrieks

At 3am this morning, inhabitants of the Rue Morgue were disturbed by a succession of horrific shrieks. The shrieks came from an apartment shared by Madame L'Espanaye and her daughter Mademoiselle Camille L'Espanaye.

Arguing

It took eight neighbours and two policemen to break through the gate and access the main building. By the time they reached the door of the L'Espanaye apartment on the fourth floor, the shrieks had stopped, to be replaced by two male voices arguing. By the time the witnesses succeeded in breaking through the door, the room was silent and nobody was there.

mutilated very badly hurt and cut about – **elderly lady** old woman
witness sb who saw sth happen – **horrific shriek** frightening scream
inhabitant sb who lives somewhere – **disturbed** stopped from doing sth
succession [sək'seʃn] *here:* a number of shrieks one afte
another – **to succeed** [sək'si:d] to manag

the Rue Morgue

A police spokesman told us that the room was in a wild disorder. The bed was broken, and money and valuable jewellery were scattered on the floor. Police found a razor, covered in blood. On the hearth they found two or three long thick tresses of grey human hair, which seemed to have been pulled out in handfuls from the roots.

Strangled

The body of the younger victim was eventually found up the chimney. She had been pushed up feet-first with great force. Her face was badly scratched, and dark bruises on her neck suggested that she had been strangled.

Fearfully Mutilated

The body of her elderly mother was found soon after, in the small paved yard to the rear of the building. Her head had been entirely severed from her body, which itself was fearfully mutilated.

Anyone who has information relating to these brutal murders should inform the Gendarmerie on Rue Montmartre. All assistance will be treated in the strictest confidence.

scattered all over the place, without order – **hearth** [hɑːθ] the floor of a fireplace in a room – **tress of hair** a long piece of hair – **root** *here: Haarwurzel* – **strangled** to be killed by sb putting their hands tightly round your neck – **chimney** *Kamin* – **rear** at the back of sth – **entirely severed** completely cut off – **assistance** help, *here:* useful information

GAZETTE DES TRIBUNAUX

Dupin was extraordinarily interested in this case. I observed him with fascination. Just as when he reads my mind, his eyes shone wildly and his voice was tense. The following morning, he rushed out to buy an early edition of the *Gazette*.

His keen interest was rewarded. The police had taken the most unusual step of providing the newspaper with details of all the witness statements they had received. This suggested that, unable to reach any conclusions themselves, they were throwing the case open to the public. Dupin's eyes blazed. He thrust the *Gazette* into my hands.

When I read the statements I was completely bemused. I've tabulated the witnesses' reports below for you. Can *you* make any sense of them? Most witnesses described two voices they heard arguing when the screaming had stopped. I have called these Voice 1 and Voice 2.

extraordinarily very – **to rush out** to leave quickly – **keen** eager – **rewarded** *belohnt* – **to provide** to give sb sth – **to blaze** to shine brightly – **to thrust** to push sth at sb – **bemused** confused, mixed-up

	Witness	Nationality	Occupation
	Pauline Duborg	French	Laundress
	Isidore Muste	French	Policeman
	Henri Duval	French	Neighbour
	Herr Odenheimer	Dutch	Restaurant owner
	William Bird	English	Tailor
	Alfonzo Garcio	Spanish	Undertaker
	Alberto Montani	Italian	Sweet shop owner
	Jules Mignaud	French	Bank manager
	Adolphe le Bon	French	Bank clerk

Observations	Description of Voice 1	Description of Voice 2
The victims were wealthy. he witness never saw any visitors at their apartment.		
elped to break into the house. The eams seemed as though somebody ; in great pain. Loud voices seemed to be arguing.	Male, gruff, French. Said 'diable', 'sacre' and 'mon dieu'.	Shrill, could be male or female. Possibly speaking Spanish.
victims had lived there for six years ıd never had visitors. The window utters were always closed, except at window of the large back room on ourth storey, where witness believes ıe ladies spent most of their time. Knew the victims well.	Male, gruff, French. Said 'diable', 'sacre' and 'mon dieu'.	Shrill, could be male or female. Definitely not the voice of either of the victims. Possibly speaking Italian.
ırieks seemed to last ten minutes. ered the house with the policemen.	Male, gruff, French. Said 'diable', 'sacre' and 'mon dieu'.	Harsh, frightened and angry. Loud and quick. Possibly speaking French.
elped to force entry into the house. rd the sounds of people struggling – scraping and shuffling.	Gruff, a Frenchman. Heard distinctly 'sacre' and 'mon dieu'.	Possibly a woman. Louder than voice 1. Definitely not English – sounded German, although Bird himself does not speak German.
	Gruff. Frenchman.	Shrill. Englishman. Mr Garcio does not speak any English. He guessed from the intonation.
	Gruff. Frenchman.	Thinks it might be Russian.
ree days before her death, Madame Espanaye took out 4,000 Francs in ld. The money was conveyed to her home by the bank's clerk.		
Three days before the murders he companied Mme L'Espanaye to her ne, with the gold in two bags. Didn't e anybody in the street. It is a very quiet back-street.		

occupation job – **laundress** sb who washes other peoples' clothes – **shutter** sth on the outside of a window, closed at night – **either** one or the other – **Dutch** from Holland (the Netherlands) – **tailor** sb who makes clothes – **to force entry** to go into sb's house without using a key – **scraping and shuffling** *here:* sound of people fighting on the floor – **distinctly** very clearly – **undertaker** sb who buries dead bodies – **conveyed** [kən'veɪd] passed or given to sb – **clerk** [klɑːk] sb who works in a bank or an office – **to accompany** to go with sb

The report included some further bewildering facts:

- The door of the room in which Mademoiselle L'Espanaye's body was found was locked from the inside.
- By the time the neighbours and policemen entered, the place was silent and empty.
- The windows of both the front and back rooms were closed and locked from the inside.
- A door between the two rooms was closed, but not locked.
- The door leading from the front room into the passage was locked, with the key on the inside.
- A small front room on the fourth storey was open and the door ajar. It was crowded with old furniture and boxes.
- The time between the arguing voices and the successful breaking down of the door was somewhere between three and five minutes.

bewildering confusing, not very clear – **passage** corridor, hall – **ajar** [ə'dʒɑː] open a little bit

- The chimneys were all too narrow for a human to pass down them.
- There is no rear entrance to the property.
- Mademoiselle L'Espanaye's body was so firmly wedged up the chimney that it took five men to pull her down.
- The money delivered by the bank clerk three days ago had not been taken. It was found on the floor in its original bags.

Dupin seemed extraordinarily interested in the affair. By good fortune, he was acquainted with the Prefect of the Police, through whom he soon succeeded in acquiring a copy of the physician's report on the two bodies.

to pass down *here:* to go down – **property** the building or house – **firmly wedged** forced into sth narrow so that you can't get it out – **affair** *here:* what was happening, the mystery – **to be acquainted with** [ə'kweɪntɪd] to know sb, to be friends with sb – **to acquire** [ə'kwaɪə] to get, to receive – **physician** [fɪ'zɪʃn] doctor

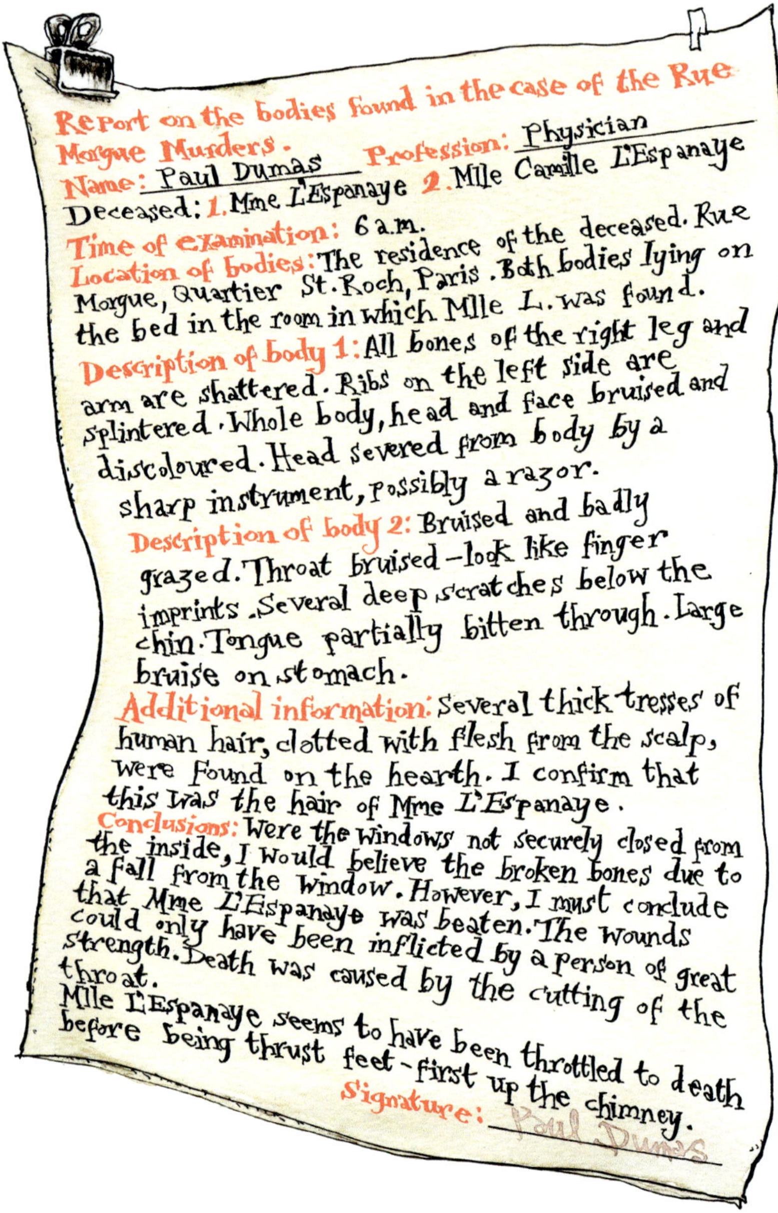

Report on the bodies found in the case of the Rue Morgue Murders.

Name: Paul Dumas Profession: Physician

Deceased: 1. Mme L'Espanaye 2. Mlle Camille L'Espanaye

Time of examination: 6 a.m.

Location of bodies: The residence of the deceased. Rue Morgue, Quartier St. Roch, Paris. Both bodies lying on the bed in the room in which Mlle L. was found.

Description of body 1: All bones of the right leg and arm are shattered. Ribs on the left side are splintered. Whole body, head and face bruised and discoloured. Head severed from body by a sharp instrument, possibly a razor.

Description of body 2: Bruised and badly grazed. Throat bruised – look like finger imprints. Several deep scratches below the chin. Tongue partially bitten through. Large bruise on stomach.

Additional information: Several thick tresses of human hair, clotted with flesh from the scalp, were found on the hearth. I confirm that this was the hair of Mme L'Espanaye.

Conclusions: Were the windows not securely closed from the inside, I would believe the broken bones due to a fall from the window. However, I must conclude that Mme L'Espanaye was beaten. The wounds could only have been inflicted by a person of great strength. Death was caused by the cutting of the throat.

Mlle L'Espanaye seems to have been throttled to death before being thrust feet-first up the chimney.

Signature: Paul Dumas

deceased [dɪ'siːst] dead – **residence** the place where sb lives – **shattered and splintered** broken so that there are only bits left – **grazed** scratched open so it bleeds – **to clot** to stick together with sth, e.g. blood – **scalp** the skin on the top of the head – **to conclude** to finish – **to inflict** to do sth (painful) to sb – **to throttle** ['θrɒtl] to hold your hands around sb's neck and shake them

Later that same day, looking up from his eagerly-acquired evening edition of the *Gazette*, Dupin told me that Adolphe le Bon, the bank clerk, had been arrested, although there did not appear to be any incriminating evidence. 'What is your opinion of these murders?' he asked me.

I confessed that I was entirely baffled.

'The police are doing a poor job,' sighed Dupin, carefully folding the paper. 'There is no method in their proceedings.' I looked at him for further explanation. 'They are impairing their vision by holding the object too close.' He was now on his feet, heading towards the door. 'Let's go and see for ourselves.'

We arrived in the Rue Morgue late in the afternoon. Dupin's previously mentioned connection with the Prefect of Police meant that we had easily obtained permission to visit the premises. Before entering, we walked up

eagerly-acquired got very quickly – **to arrest** to take sb to the police station and not let them go – **incriminating evidence** facts or information that show sb has done sth – **to confess** to admit – **baffled** ['bæfld] speechless, amazed – **to impair sb's vision** to make it not easy for sb to see sth – **to obtain permission** to get sb to let you do sth – **premises** building, house

the street, turned down an alley and round to the rear of the building. As we walked, Dupin examined the whole area with an attention to detail for which I could see no obvious reason. He remained silent.

Entering the building, we went straight upstairs to the room in which the bodies still lay. Dupin scrutinised everything, including the bodies, in such minute detail that it was dark by the time we left. All the way home, he declined to discuss the murders.

alley ['æli] a small lane or road – **to scrutinise** ['skruːtɪnaɪz] to look at everything very carefully – **minute** [maɪ'njuːt] very small – **to decline** to not be willing to do sth

It wasn't until noon the next day, as we sat together at home, that he suddenly asked me, 'Did you observe anything *peculiar* yesterday?'

Something in the way he emphasised 'peculiar' made me shudder. I answered that I had seen nothing more than was reported in the *Gazette*.

'But the *Gazette* has not entered into the unusual horror of the murders. This horror, which so confounds the police, should make the case easy to solve. They are also puzzled by the different descriptions of the voices, and by the fact that nobody was discovered upstairs, even though there could have been no escape without passing those ascending the stairs. These factors should lead us towards a conclusion, not away from one. We should not ask "What has occurred?" but "What has occurred that has never occurred before?" This is what has led me to the solution of this mystery.'

peculiar [pɪˈkjuːliə] strange, odd, unusual – **shudder** *Schaudern* – **to enter into** *here:* to explain in detail

The solution? I was astonished. How could these strange factors, so bewildering to me, already have led Dupin to a conclusion? If you remember what I told you earlier of his analytical skill, you may not be surprised by his progress. Maybe you have been able to find a solution as quickly as Dupin, but I expect you are as lost as I was.

I stared at my friend in mute astonishment.

'I am now awaiting somebody,' he said. I continued to stare. Dupin read the increased anxiety in my face. 'I am not awaiting the murderer himself,' he reassured me, 'but a person who must have been implicated in the events in the Rue Morgue. He may not arrive, but if he does it will be necessary to detain him.'

Dupin handed me one of two pistols, which I took eagerly. He then began to lead me, step by meticulously-detailed step, through

astonished amazed, surprised – **progress** *Fortschritt* – **mute astonishment** so surprised you can't say anything – **to increase** to become greater – **to reassure** to make sb feel better or more sure – **to be implicated** to be involved – **to detain** [dɪˈteɪn] to keep, to arrest – **meticulously** [məˈtɪkjələsli] very carefully

the process by which he had reached his conclusion. To him, the workings of my own mind must have seemed excessively laborious. I wonder whether you will fare any better. You have a slight advantage over me, as I have placed Dupin's reasoning below in tabular form, whereas I had to listen very carefully to his complicated explanation.

workings of sth the way sth works – **excessively laborious** *here:* very slow – **to fare** to get on – **slight** little, small – **tabular** made into a table or grid

Evidence

The two voices heard after the screams were definitely not the voices of the deceased ladies.

When the witnesses broke in, the murderer(s) were no longer there.

The doors were locked from the inside. The chimneys were too narrow for a human body to get through. No secret exits were found. The windows appeared to be fastened shut.

If the murderer(s) had escaped via a door or a front window, they would have been seen by the crowd who had rushed up the stairs.

The rear windows appeared to be nailed shut from the inside.

Upon close examination, Dupin discovered that the nails were attached to concealed springs, which thrust them into the wood when the sash windows slid into their closed positions.

If we accept that the window was open, we must assume that Mme L'Espanaye's body was thrown from it.

This small part of the mystery I acknowledged solved. The murderer had entered and exited via a window which had then slid closed, a locking mechanism springing into place. But the window in question was four storeys above

exit way out – **fastened shut** closed and locked – **via** by way of – **to rush up** to go up sth very fast – **nailed shut** *festgenagelt* – **concealed spring** *versteckte Feder* – **to slide into** to move into – **to acknowledge** [ək'nɒlɪdʒ] to accept, to understand – **to spring into place** *einrasten*

Conclusion
The murders were perpetrated by a third party – at least two others being involved.
They were not ghosts or spirits, so they must have found a physical means of escape.
These are the only escape options. Although escape seems impossible, it must somehow have been possible. Therefore, one of these must not be as it seems.
They escaped via a rear window.
This must not be the case, as they are the only possible exit. The windows therefore have the power of fastening themselves.
One of the windows must have slid closed, and the nail sprung across to lock it after the murderer(s) escaped.
Mme L'Espanaye's broken bones and bruises were caused by the fall, not, as the physician concluded, by a severe beating.

the ground. 'I see that your next question is that of the mode of ascent and descent,' Dupin read my mind. 'Upon this point I satisfied myself when we walked around the back of the building before we entered.'

perpetrated done – **fastening** fixing, staying open or closed – **to spring across** to close, to move across – **severe beating** being hit by sb or sth very hard lots of times – **ascent** [ə'sent] going up – **descent** [dɪ'sent] going down

Evidence	Conclusion
About 1.5 metres from the window in question there runs a lightning rod. The wooden shutters of the window are particularly wide. If swung fully back to the wall, one would reach to within about 75 centimetres of the lightning rod.	The murderer must have climbed the rod, grasped the lattice of the shutter and, pushing against the wall with his feet, swung the shutter closed and sprung himself through the window and into the room. He could have exited by the reverse of this procedure.
At the foot of the lightning rod, Dupin found a piece of ribbon tied in a knot so complicated that few besides sailors could have tied it.	As yet, no conclusion.

lightning rod *Blitzableiter* – **to swing fully back** to move all the way back – **to grasp** to hold onto – **lattice** [ˈlætɪs] pieces of wood going across the shutter – **reverse** doing sth backwards – **ribbon** thin piece of cloth – **besides** other than

'I wish to impress upon you,' said Dupin, 'the almost superhuman strength and agility required to carry out this acrobatic feat. This is important. Remember – it is the strange things that happened in spite of their improbability which make this case so easy to solve.'

I don't know how you the reader are getting on, but I was not, at this point, finding it particularly easy.

Dupin now invited me to consider further the witness reports of the voices heard arguing in the apartment. 'The witnesses, you will have observed, were all in agreement about the gruff voice. They knew that it was French, and they could identify particular words.'

'Yes,' I acknowledged this to be true, 'but there was much disagreement in regard to the second, shrill voice.'

to impress upon to tell sb how important sth is – **superhuman** having abilities a normal human does not have – **agility** the ability of moving quickly – **required** needed – **to carry out** to do sth – **feat** [fiːt] thing, act – **improbability** unlikeliness, not likely

Evidence	Conclusion
Not only did the witnesses disagree on the language spoken by the second voice, but all of them identified the speaker as a foreigner. Amongst those witnesses, who between them represented most of the great languages of Europe, not one was able to identify the language as his own.	It could have been an Asian or an African language, or a less-well-known European language such as Estonian, Russian or Icelandic.
There are very few people in Paris who speak these less well known languages.	We might still consider this a possibility, but its improbability must also be allowed.
The voice was described by one witness as 'harsh rather than shrill,' and by two others as 'quick and unequal.' No individual words were distinguishable.	At this point, the strangeness of the voice must be accepted as a fact. It should therefore contribute to a conclusion.

foreigner sb from another country – **amongst** with all – **less-well-known** not known by many people – **distinguishable** *here:* could clearly be heard

Dupin summarised his conclusions so far. 'I wish you to bear in mind the evidence we now have of the unusual degree of strength, agility and courage shown in entering and departing from the room, alongside the strange nature of the voice.' This gave me a vague, half-formed idea. I was on the verge of understanding without being able to understand. It felt the same as those occasions when you are on the brink of remembering something, like a person's name for example, but just cannot grasp the memory.

Dupin then began to explain the further conclusions he had been able to draw from the appearance of the rooms when we arrived.

to summarise to express the most important facts in a few words – **to bear in mind** to think about – **alongside** as well as – **verge of** close to – **brink of** close to – **to grasp the memory** to remember sth

Evidence	Conclusion
The drawers of the bureau had been rifled, but it seemed that nothing had been taken. The four thousand francs in gold, brought by the bank clerk three days earlier, was discovered in its original bags on the floor.	If theft had been the motive, only an idiot would have abandoned both the gold and the motive. The fact that the gold was delivered three days before the murders is merely coincidence. We are therefore without a motive.
The murders were atrocious and unusual. One body was thrust feet-first up a chimney. Mme L'Espanaye's head was completely severed from its body by a mere razor, and a whole fistful of hair, and its roots, had been pulled from her head.	What murderer could be so strong, or so depraved? For such unusual murders, an unusual answer must be sought.

drawer *Schublade* – **bureau** *(old)* desk – **to rifle** to go through sth, to search – **to abandon** to leave behind – **merely** ['mɪəli] only – **coincidence** [kəʊ'ɪnsɪdəns] events that happen at the same time but are not connected – **atrocious** awful, horrible, frightening – **depraved** mad, not clear in the head – **to seek, sought** ['sɔːt] to look for

'What impression has this made upon you?' Dupin asked me.

My flesh creeping, I replied, 'I can only think that a madman, or some raving maniac escaped from a neighbouring asylum, could have committed the murders.'

'Your idea is not irrelevant,' said Dupin, 'but now take a look at this.' He held out a tuft of coarse, tawny-coloured hair. 'I disentangled this from the rigidly clenched fingers of Mme L'Espanaye.'

It was not human hair.

to make one's flesh creep *eine Gänsehaut bekommen* – **raving** complete – **asylum** hospital for mad people – **tuft** *here:* handful – **coarse** rough, not flat – **tawny** light brown – **to disentangle** *here:* to take out of carefully – **clenched** held firmly shut

Dupin then showed me some measurements he had taken of the bruises on Mlle L'Espanaye's neck, and invited me to measure my own hand against them. I made the attempt in vain. The marks were too far apart. 'This,' I said, 'is the mark of no human hand.'

mark *Abdruck* – **far apart** not close together

'Now read this,' said Dupin, passing me a book by Cuvier, a famous French zoologist. It was open on a page describing the orang-utan of the East Indies: a strong and ferocious creature. I understood the full horrors of the murders at once. I imagine that you have too.

The murders themselves might now have been solved, but I was still puzzled by the accounts of the two voices. Dupin explained further. 'A Frenchman was witness to, or arrived just after the murders. His exclamation of "Mon dieu" was one of horror. It is only a guess, but it is likely that the creature had escaped from the Frenchman's care prior to committing the murders.' He then handed me a copy of a newspaper called *Le Monde*, popular with sailors. 'I have placed an advertisement in the paper. It should bring the Frenchman to our residence,' he said.

ferocious nasty, biting, fighting – **exclamation** shout – **care** looking after – **prior** ['praɪə] before

Remembering the pistol in my hand, I laid it on the table, took the paper and read Dupin's advertisement.

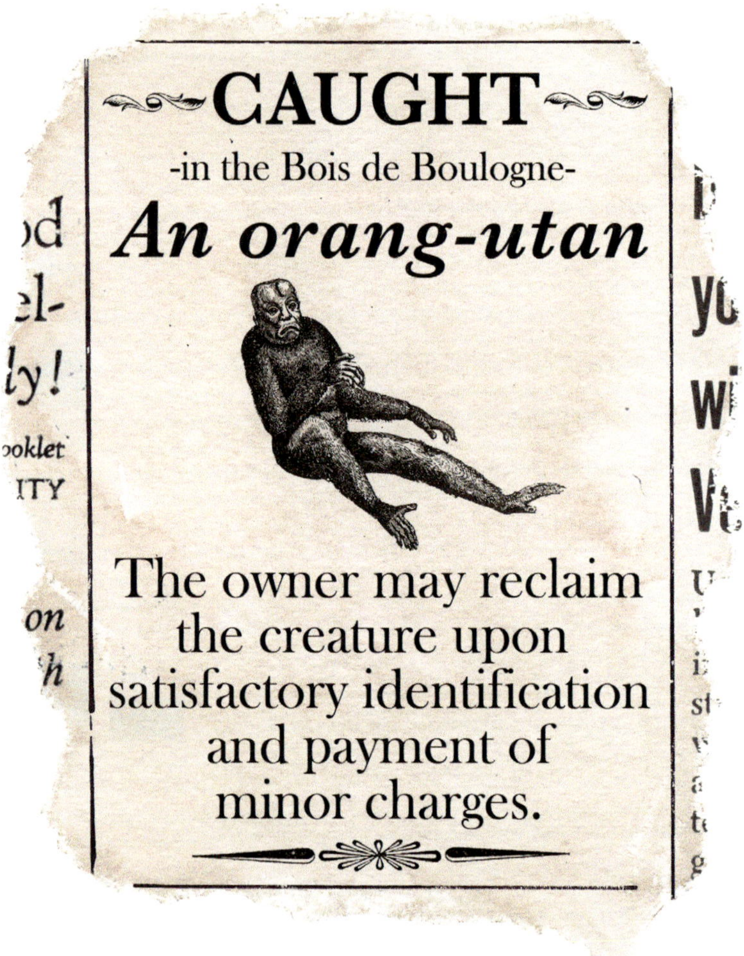

to reclaim [rɪˈkleɪm] to get back – **payment** giving of money – **minor charge** small amount of money

It then gave our address.

'I am not sure that this will work,' admitted Dupin, 'but the knotted ribbon I found suggests that the Frenchman in question was a sailor, who had captured the beast on one of his voyages, in the hope of profiting from his sale. I have said that the creature was found in the Bois de Boulogne, a long way from here, so that the sailor will not believe his beast to be suspected of the murders. He is therefore more likely to come to collect him.'

At that moment we heard a footstep outside, followed by a rapping at the door. I picked up my pistol and hid it behind my back.

'Come in,' said Dupin, in a cheerful tone.

A tall, muscular man entered. His sunburnt face, half-hidden by beard and moustache, confirmed him as a sailor. He bowed awkwardly and bade us good evening in an accent which confirmed him as a native Frenchman.

to capture to catch – **voyage** ['vɔɪɪdʒ] long journey on a boat – **suspected** thought of – **to rap** to knock hard on sth – **cheerful** happy – **moustache** [mə'stɑːʃ] line of hair between nose and mouth – **to bow** [baʊ] to move your head and body forward and down – **to bade** to greet, to say – **native** coming from a country

'Sit down, my friend,' said Dupin. 'Your orang-utan is a remarkably fine creature and no doubt very valuable.'

'Have you got him here?' asked the Frenchman, looking nervously around. 'I am very willing to pay you a reward for finding him.'

'Well,' replied Dupin. 'Let me think – what reward should I have? Oh! I know! As my reward you shall tell me everything you know about the murders in the Rue Morgue.'

The sailor flushed and started to his feet, before falling back into his chair, trembling violently. I pitied him from the bottom of my heart.

'My friend,' said Dupin in a kind tone, 'I pledge you the honour of a gentleman that we intend you no injury. You are not guilty of the murders, but you are bound by every principle of honour to reveal all that you know. An innocent man is now imprisoned, charged with this crime.'

I remembered the unfortunate bank clerk.

remarkably very – **reward** money sb gets for giving back lost things – **to flush** to go red – **to pity** to feel sorry for sb – **honour** ['ɒnə] *Ehre* – **to intend** to want, to plan – **bound** tied – **to reveal** [rɪ'viːl] to tell, to make sth known – **innocent** not guilty – **charged** officially found guilty of a crime by the police

'So help me God,' said the sailor, recovering his presence of mind. 'I *am* innocent, and I *will* tell you all that I know.'

Your analytical faculties having been exercised by this story, and your desire to hear the concluding pieces of evidence being probably strong, I will present to you the sailor's story in linear form. This seems most suitable for our present state of mind.

He captured the orang-utan in Borneo. He brought it home and kept it secretly in his home in Paris, until such a time as he could sell it. He came home one evening to find that the creature had escaped from its bonds and, its face covered in shaving foam, was trying to imitate the action of shaving, razor in hand. The sailor seized his whip in an attempt to capture the creature. Terrified, and still clutching the razor, the creature fled into the open street. The sailor gave chase.

to recover to get back – **presence of mind** *here:* feeling normal – **desire** wanting – **bonds** ties, ropes, chains – **shaving foam** *Rasierschaum* – **to seize** [siːz] to take hold of sth quickly – **whip** *Peitsche* – **to clutch** [klʌtʃ] to hold onto sth

The creature ran into the Rue Morgue, where its attention was caught by a light gleaming from an open window on the fourth floor. It climbed into the window as surmised by Dupin. The sailor easily climbed the lightning rod, but was unable to swing on the shutter. All that he could do was reach over far enough to catch a glimpse of the room's interior. He was horrified by what he saw.

The screams of the two ladies turned the creature from peaceful and curious to terrified and angry. The more it attacked, the more the ladies screamed, and the more frenzied it became. When the ladies were dead, it seemed conscious of having done wrong. To conceal its crimes, it thrust the younger lady up the chimney and flung the elder from the window. At this point the sailor fled, abandoning in his terror all concern for the beast.

to gleam to shine – **to surmise** ['sɜːmaɪz] to guess – **glimpse** a quick look – **interior** [ɪn'tɪəriə] inside – **horrified** frightened, scared, afraid – **frenzied** mad – **conscious** ['kɒntʃəs] aware of – **to conceal** [kən'siːl] to hide – **concern** worry, thought

There is little more to add. The orang-utan must have escaped from the room as Dupin described. The sailor eventually captured his creature, and sold him for a very large sum. The bank clerk was released from prison. The Prefect of Police could not conceal his displeasure that Dupin had solved the mystery where he himself had so completely failed. 'People really ought to mind their own business,' he complained bitterly.

'Let him complain,' said Dupin. 'It will ease his conscience. In truth, it is no surprise that he failed in the solution of this mystery, for he is somewhat too cunning to be profound. His wisdom is all head and no body, for he seeks to ignore that which is, and to explain that which is not.'

And so, I return my attention to you, the reader. You will acknowledge that Dupin succeeded because he paid close attention to

displeasure unhappiness – **mind one's own business** do one's own thing and ignore others – **bitterly** nastily, sadly – **conscience** ['kɒntʃənts] *Gewissen* – **cunning** clever – **profound** *tiefgehend* – **wisdom** knowledge – **to pay close attention** to look at sth carefully every piece of evidence, accepting it as fact and working from there, just as when he read my mind. This is how an analytical mind works.

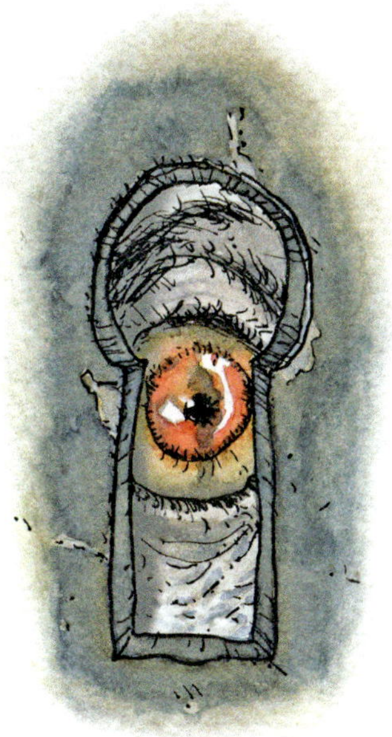

How close did you come to solving the murders in the Rue Morgue? Were you ever a step ahead of Dupin? Somehow I suspect not, unless you too are an analytic genius.

step ahead *Schritt voraus* – **to suspect** to think, to believe – **genius** a very clever person

ABOUT THE AUTHOR

Edgar Allan Poe

Edgar Allan Poe was born in Boston Massachusetts on January 19th, 1809. He died at the very young age of 40 in Baltimore on October 7th, 1849.

He was an American author, poet, editor and book critic. His books were known for being full of mystery and murders. He was one of the earliest American writers of shorts stories and was one of the first authors of detective and science fiction stories.

His American father left the family when Poe was still young. A year later his British mother died. He was looked after by John and Frances Allan, of Richmond, Virginia. They never legally adopted him but out of respect, Edgar took up *Allan* as a middle name. In 1835 he married his 13-year-old cousin, who died from tuberculosis 12 years later.

Poe was educated in Britain where the family lived for several years. When the family moved back to Richmond, Poe studied at the University of

Virginia. However, he dropped out of university after only one year because of money problems. Poe also served in the army and was a cadet at West Point, the US Military Academy. He quit this career after just three years.

Poe's first published poems were not successful. He tried to live on writing alone but he couldn't earn a living from just writing stories. He started writing texts for different magazines and newspapers, worked as an editor and was well known as a critic. He won a prize for his short story *MS. Found in a Bottle* in 1833. *The Murders in the Rue Morgue* (1841) has been recognized as the first detective story. His poem *The Raven* published in 1845 is one of his greatest works.

It is unknown what Poe died of. Speculations include alcohol or drugs, heart disease, or even suicide. However, the actual cause of death remains a mystery.

The Mystery Writers of America has an award named the *Edgar Award* which is presented annually to writers of exceptional mystery stories.

PRE-READING TASKS

1. Have you read a murder mystery novel before? What do you expect to happen in a murder story? What do you have to do when you read a murder story? Is it easy to read? It is useful to have a notebook and make notes as you read the novel so that you can remember details that are important.

2. Look at the title of this novel. In which country do you think the murders take place? What do you know about this country that makes it different to Germany and England? Will this change how you read the story? In what way? What do you expect?

3. Who do you expect the main characters in this novel to be? Think about the important people when there is a murder. What other things are important when a murder has taken place?

WHILE-READING TASKS

1. Collect information about where the murders took place. Think about:
   - the size and height of the building
   - what the apartment looks like
   - where the building is

   Draw a picture to show the apartment and the area it is in.

2. Make character cards for all the people in the book (even the two people who were murdered). Add details as you read the story.

3. If you had been the police what would you have done differently to find out who the murderer was?

4. If you had lived in the building where the murders took place and you heard the voices what would you have done?

5. Look at the newspaper report on pages 18 and 19. Look for the key information and put it into a table. Compare your table with your partner's table. Has she/he got the same information

as you or did she/he find other things more important?

6. Use the information in the table on pages 22 and 23 and the facts on pages 24 and 25 to write a description of the suspect(s) and look for a motive for the murders. There were two people in the room (two voices were heard). Were they both the murderers? What other characteristics has/have the suspect(s)? What questions about the murders still haven't been answered? Make a list.

7. Look at the doctor's report on page 26. Put the information about the two bodies into a table or take notes about them. Look at the differences between the two bodies and see how the different injuries are described. Is special language used for the descriptions? Use the information to add more details to your description of the suspect(s) in task 6. Does this information change who the suspect(s) could be?

8. On pages 32, 33, 34, 37 and 39 there are more tables comparing the evidence and the conclusions that were drawn from this evidence. Look at all the different pieces of evidence. Try and organise these tables differently. You can use cards or a mind map to help you. Do you agree with the conclusions that were drawn? Did you find more evidence when you were reading the novel that is missing? What conclusions have you drawn while reading the novel?

9. Look at the pictures again in *The Murders in Rue Morgue*. What do you think of them? Did they help you understand the story? Were they clear? What do you think of the style of them? Do they go with the style of the novel?

10. Choose a part of the story where there isn't a picture. Think about what you would include in a picture to go with this part of the story. Draw a picture with all the things in it to make this part of the story clearer.

QUESTIONS ON THE STORY

1. What puzzles and games are listed on p 7?
2. What are the tips about on p 12?
3. What was the name of the newspaper that the report about the murders was in? (p 17)
4. What was unusual about the newspaper report the following day? (p 21)
5. How did Dupin get a copy of the doctor's report on the dead bodies? (p 25)
6. What did Dupin do after he had given the narrator a pistol? (p 30)
7. What were the three things that all the witnesses were in agreement with? (p 36)
8. Who did the narrator think the murderer was? (p 41)
9. What did the owner of the orang-utan have to do to get it back? (p 44)
10. What did the sailor do after he had seen what the orang-utan had done? (p 50)

POST-READING TASKS

1. What puzzling mysteries in everyday life can you think of that you would like to know the answers to?

2. Look on the Internet and find out about other novels by Edgar Allan Poe. What sort of novels are they? Which of his other novels would you like to read? What about your friends, which ones would interest them?

3. Which other authors do you know who write detective novels? Which novels have you read? What did you think of them?

4. Was the novel easy to read? The narrator asks lots of questions and explains lots of things that aren't directly about the murders. Did you find this good or was it annoying? Did it help you when reading *The Murders in the Rue Morgue*?

5. Who did you think the murderer was? Were you right? Why did you think this person was the murderer? Did you change your mind while

reading the novel? Were you surprised when you found out who had murdered the two women?

6. Who was your favourite character in *The Murders in the Rue Morgue*? Why did you like this character the most?

7. This story is a shortened version of the original book by Edgar Allan Poe. When you read the story were there parts where you felt there was information missing? Do you think this is where the story was shortened? Do you think the story would be better if there was more information in it?

8. Is it a good idea that well-known books are shortened and made easier for younger readers? Are there other famous stories that you would like to read but you think they are too hard for you?

9. How often did you think you knew who the murderer was and then changed your mind? When and why did you change your mind?

How often did you change your mind? What made you sure in the end that you were right?

10. *The Murders in the Rue Morgue* was made into a TV film in 1986. Find the film and watch it. What did you think of the film? Was it like the book? Did you prefer it to the book?

ABBREVIATIONS USED IN ANNOTATIONS AND TASKS

e.g.	exempli gratia; for example
inf	informal
old	old-fashioned
p	page
sb	somebody
sth	something